# HORRIBLE
# HISTORIES

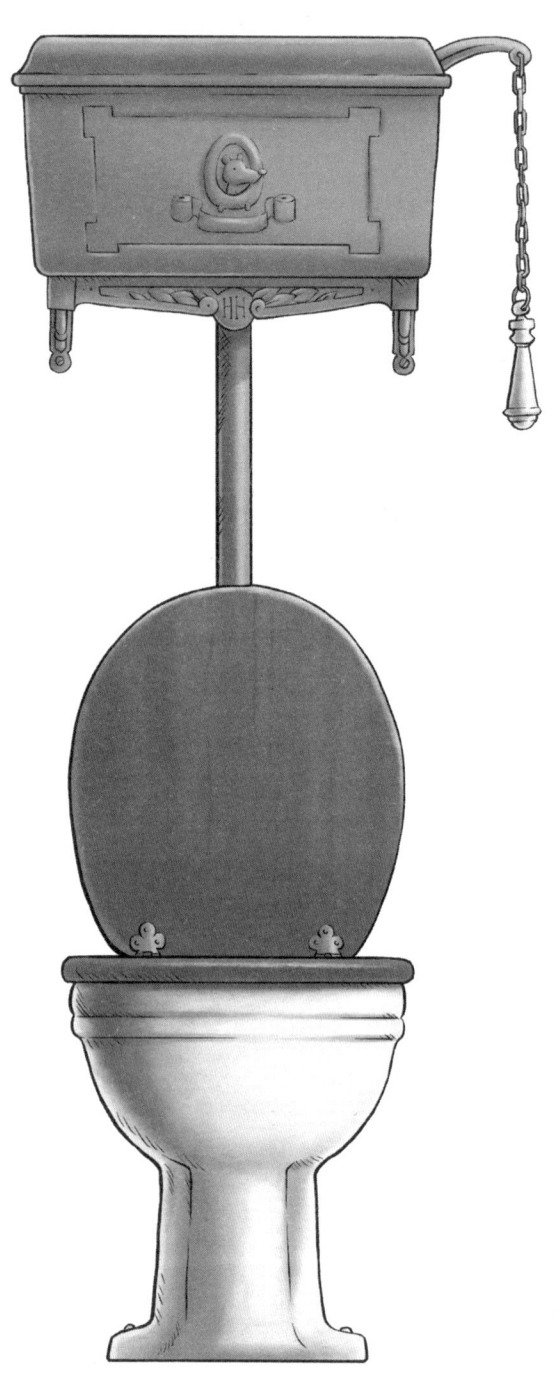

# HORRIBLE HISTORIES

# The Truly Terrible History of the Toilet

ILLUSTRATED BY
TERRY DEARY ✤ MARTIN BROWN

■ SCHOLASTIC

For Sian Jones – the bestest niece in the world. TD

To everyone reading this – on the loo. MB

Published in the UK by Scholastic, 2024
Scholastic, Bosworth Avenue, Warwick, CV34 6UQ
Scholastic Ireland, 89E Lagan Road, Dublin Industrial Estate, Glasnevin, Dublin, D11 HP5F

SCHOLASTIC and associated logos are trademarks and/or
registered trademarks of Scholastic Inc.

Text © Terry Deary, 2024
Cover illustration © Martin Brown, 2024

The moral rights of the author and illustrator have been asserted by them.

ISBN 978 0702 33743 7

A CIP catalogue record for this book is available from the British Library.

All rights reserved.
This book is sold subject to the condition that it shall not, by way of trade or otherwise, be lent, hired out or otherwise circulated in any form of binding or cover other than that in which it is published. No part of this publication may be reproduced, stored in a retrieval system, or transmitted in any form or by any other means (electronic, mechanical, photocopying, recording or otherwise) or used to train any artificial intelligence technologies without prior written permission of Scholastic Limited. Subject to EU law Scholastic Limited expressly reserves this work from the text and data mining exception.

Printed in the UK
Paper made from wood grown in sustainable forests and other controlled sources.

10 9 8 7 6 5 4 3 2

www.scholastic.co.uk

For safety or quality concerns:
UK: www.scholastic.co.uk/productinformation
EU: www.scholastic.ie/productinformation

# CONTENTS

Introduction **7**
The Ancients **11**
Measly Middle Ages **26**
Terrifying Tudors **59**
Slimy Stuarts **73**
Gorgeous Georgians **82**
Vile Victorians **93**
The First and Second World Wars **104**
Terrible Toilet Tales **116**
Toilet Rolls **125**
Super Sewers **133**
E-pee-log **148**
Interesting Index **154**

# INTRODUCTION

People are scared of sharks…

But there are far greater dangers in the world.
In 1984 an American said...

Panic spread. In Queensland, Australia, one area pulled down all the coconut trees on its beaches. In Honolulu signs were put up warning people about death by cruel coconuts.

Millions of people around the world believe that killer coconuts crush 150 heads. But this is a Horrible Histories book and Horrible Histories tells you the TRUTH. In 1984 a hospital in Papua New Guinea wrote a report. It said TWO people were killed by coconuts. A lot more were killed by falling as they tried to climb coconut palm trees. They were mostly children. (And ONE was injured when he kicked a coconut palm tree.)

No, don't believe that nonsense. Far deadlier than sharks are something you use every day. Toilets.

And many more are injured. All through history toilets have been killing humans. Some have died in weird and horrible ways.

What the world needs is a book that tells people about the dangers. A book about the deaths and pain and misery toilets have caused. The world needs a book called *Horrible Histories: Toilets*.

But first, a *Horrible Histories* warning...

# THE ANCIENTS

# GO WHERE YOU WANT

The first humans, like dogs, just pooped wherever they wanted to. Unlike pets, they didn't pee against the nearest lamppost because lampposts hadn't been invented. The pet pooches had to make do with trees…

When humans started to gather in caves or villages they needed tidier toilets, so they dug holes in the ground. At least it went back into the ground to feed the flowers.

And, thousands of years later, modern humans discovered the pits of dried-up poo and were very excited...

'Dried-up poo' doesn't sound like a good name for science teachers when talking about ancient discoveries. So, they called these finds 'coprolites'.

Why are they exciting? Because we can tell what plants or animals the humans ate by looking at coprolites under a microscope.

First you have to soak them for three days before examining the stuff. A bit like a teabag. Just thought you might like to know that.

The volcano Vesuvius erupted in AD 79 and buried Pompeii. A town to the west of the eruption, Herculaneum, was covered in ash at first and the people had time to run away. They grabbed their precious things, but they left their poo behind in their toilet pits.

A thousand years before Herculaneum was destroyed, the ancient Egyptians had some of the first proper toilets. They were still pits in the ground, but had raised seats made of limestone. Each seat had a hole in it. The waste would fall into a pit and be covered with sand or ash.

Of course, the pharaohs didn't dig their own pits, they got some poor peasant to do it for them.

# STONE-AGE INVENTORS

Some historians say the Scots came up with a toilet that used water to flush away the waste. That was in a Stone Age village from around 3000 BC.

Others say the Greeks built the Palace of Knossos in around 1700 BC with large pans made of pottery and joined to a flushing water supply.

They were fresher than a hole in the ground. But who had the idea first?

# ROMAN EM-POO-RERS

Roman cities had thousands of people who crowded into the temples, the shops and the arenas where thousands of humans and animals were slaughtered for fun.

These ruthless Romans couldn't all run home when they had to go. They needed 'public toilets' that anyone could use.

The most common type of Roman toilet was the 'latrine'. Latrines were large rooms with rows of holes in the ground and wooden seats over the holes. About a dozen people could sit there, side by side.

When you had finished you'd clean yourself with a sponge on the end of a stick. It was called a 'tersorium', which is Latin for 'a wiping thing'. It was shared by people using public latrines. To clean the sponge, you washed it in a bucket or sink with saltwater or vinegar water. Then you passed the sponge on to the next person who wanted it.

You might not like the idea, but germs loved it, and those sponges could carry all sorts of diseases, such as typhoid. Tapeworms in the gut of one person could be passed on to the next person who then carried the worms home to share with the family. Lovely.

# TERSORIUM

THE SPONGE-ON-A-STICK MUST-HAVE BATHROOM ACCESSORY FOR EVERY BEAUTIFUL BOTTY

## WIPE YOUR BUM THE ROMAN WAY!

- NEW AND IMPROVED ORIGINAL DESIGN
- SPONGE-AND-STICK COLOURED
- HUNDREDS OF HAPPY PREVIOUS USERS
- MCLXX FLIES CAN'T BE WRONG
- NO JOB TOO SMALL
- ONE SIZE FITS ALL

**RECYCLE AND REUSE**

SIMPLY
## WIPE, RINSE AND PASS IT ON!
## AGAIN
AND
## AGAIN
AND
## AGAIN!

ABSOLUTELY NO ANTI-BACTERIAL OR ANTI-VIRAL PROPERTIES WHATSOEVER

# DID YOU KNOW...?

Around AD 50 the Roman writer Seneca reported that a German gladiator killed himself with a tersorium sponge on a stick. The gladiator didn't want to face death in the arena watched by cheering and jeering thousands. So, he hid himself in the latrine and pushed the wooden stick down his throat until he choked to death.

---

Latrines were often placed next to Roman baths. The bathers could use them before or after bathing and the bathwater was used to flush the toilets.

The Romans took the idea of sewers from the ancient Etruscan people around 500 BC. The waste from their latrines dropped into a small sewer and was washed away with a stream of water into a bigger sewer.

But rats, snakes and spiders would live in those sewers too. Rich people didn't want rats (and smells) in their own homes, so they used pots as toilets. Enslaved people carried them outside and emptied the pots into a pool, away from the house. The pool – what we call a 'cesspit' – was emptied from time to time and the waste was spread on the land to help the crops to grow. Poor people who used pots had to dig their own holes. A Roman law was passed to say…

**EMPTY YOUR TOILET POTS WITH CARE**

IF YOU TIP YOUR POT OUT OF YOUR WINDOW IN DAYTIME – AND IT HITS SOMEONE IN THE STREET – YOU MUST PAY TO HAVE THEIR CLOTHES CLEANED.
AT NIGHT YOU MAY TIP WHATEVER YOU LIKE.

If you were walking the dark streets of Rome at night you were probably up to no good. If you were hit by human waste it served you right.

Dirty sewers let the waste rot and give off a gas called methane – it was very explosive if a flame came near. That would blow you off your toilet seat.

Some of these sewers were so large you could drive a horse pulling a cartload of hay through them. These sewers flowed into the River Tiber, where fish fed on the waste. The fish were then caught and eaten by the Romans. Tasty.

Rome's sewers had one very nasty bit of waste shoved down. An emperor. The evil emperor Elagabalus (reigned AD 218 to 222) was cruel as a crocodile with toothache. He...

✹ Ordered a servant to gather a huge weight of cobwebs. When the man returned empty-handed, Elagabalus shut him in a cage and he was eaten alive by dozens of starving rats.

✹ Had a team of enslaved women strapped into a chariot to pull him around his gardens as he whipped them.

✹ Sacrificed children to his favourite Roman god and forced their parents to watch as their guts were spilled.

✹ Invented an early sort of whoopee cushion for guests at his banquets. When they sat on the padded couches they gave out a loud 'parp'. A sort of wind in the pillows.

- Had feasts where guests ate camel heels, flamingo brains, tongues of nightingales and a delightful dish of cooked parrot heads.

The Romans soon grew tired of him, and a historian wrote of what happened next…

> Elagabalus attempted to flee the assassins that came for him. He almost got away by hiding in a chest in a toilet. But he was discovered and slain, at the age of 18. His mother, who hugged and clung tightly to him, died with him. Their heads were cut off and their bodies, after being stripped naked, were first dragged all over the city and then stuffed into a sewer.

The sewer was too narrow, and his body wouldn't flush away, so his corpse was thrown into the Tiber. The dead emperor's friends were tortured, and wooden stakes driven through them.

# NASTY NERO

Another evil emperor was Nero (reigned AD 54 to 68). Nero's idea of a fun night out was to walk the streets of Rome disguised as a common man. He would then attack strangers and beat them.

He was a bit of a coward because he knew there were bodyguards watching his back. If a beating went wrong, and Nero looked like getting hurt, then the guards would jump into the fight to save the emperor.

If a beating was too vicious then the stranger would be knocked out cold. That was when Nero would stuff the poor victim's body into one of Rome's famous sewers.

# WEE ON THE WEAVE

If you wanted clean clothes in Ancient Rome then you would take them to the cleaners. It was a job you wouldn't want to do yourself.

🌸 The Germans had soap, but the Romans stuck to the old ways to keep clothes clean … 'fullers earth' (clay) kept fine material like cotton free of grease. But tougher material like wool would be cleaned with a mixture of potash (plant ashes soaked in water) and urine.

🌸 The cleaners would collect urine from public pee pots placed on street corners. They were less keen on pee from pub toilets as its nitrogen content was too low. Those Roman cleaners knew their urine. They trampled the cloth in the urine mixture, often while live music was being played for them.

🟣 Posh togas could be made a brilliant white by steaming them in sulphur. This also made them highly flammable – like walking around dressed in the head of a match. Keep away from naked flames or end up as match of the day.

# NAME THAT TOILET: KHAZI

Some people feel it's a bit disgusting to say the word 'toilet', so they come up with new words. You may like to try some of these on your teachers when you are in class and need to go. Just don't blame *Horrible Histories* if the teacher is shocked and gives you a thousand hours of detention. Or – worse – gives you a history lesson...

# MEASLY MIDDLE AGES

## NAME THAT TOILET:
# THRONE

........................................................

Calling a toilet a 'throne' is meant to be a joke because, as you know, kings and queens sit on thrones. But one king got a nasty shock when he sat on the toilet.

# KILLER TOILETS

........................................................

On 30 November 1016, King Edmund II was killed. He'd only worn the crown for a few months, but the Viking King Cnut wanted to rule England. Edmund was such a brave English warrior he was known as 'Ironsides'. But it wasn't his sides that needed iron. It was his bum.

One night Edmund Ironside went to the toilet, which was a pit covered by a wooden seat. Little did he know that an earl, Eadric Streona, had sent an assassin to lie in wait for him. Streona means 'grasper' and Eadric loved to grasp lands and riches.

Eadric had married Edmund's sister, and had helped to kill off the enemies of his father-in-law, King Ethelred. Then in 1015 he switched sides and fought for the Viking King Cnut.

EDMUND II WAS CNUT'S BIGGEST ENEMY. I THOUGHT CNUT WOULD BE PLEASED IF I BUMPED HIM OFF

The assassin sent by Eadric Streona sneaked into King Edmund's camp and hid in the toilet pit. He waited till King Edmund sat on the toilet seat.

The assassin struck upwards twice with his long knife and Edmund fell off his throne. Dead. The killer rushed off to tell Eadric and Cnut what he had done … but he probably had a wash first, after all that poop and blood had covered him.

Cnut was not pleased that Edmund had been murdered in such a shocking way. He had Eadric's head cut off and stuck on top of the tallest tree in the forest.

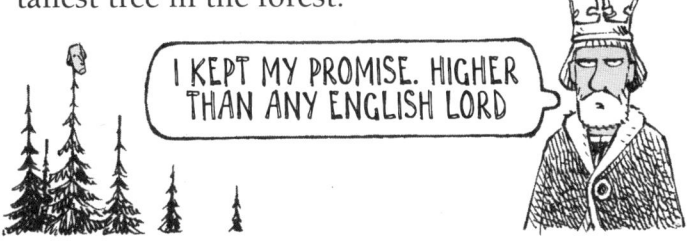

That's the story told by historian Henry of Huntingdon. Other writers say Edmund Ironside was poisoned.

The French writer Geoffrey Gaimar wrote that Edmund was killed with a booby-trapped crossbow hidden in the toilet pit. It fired a bolt into his bum when he sat down.

# KILLER TOILETS 2

One story that MAY be true is the death of King George II in 1760. He ordered the last ever beheading at the Tower of London. He died after breakfast. Horace Walpole wrote:

> *King George rose as usual at six and drank his chocolate as this was one of his many habits. At quarter past seven he went into a little closet. His German servant waited for him. The servant heard a noise, and ran in. He found the King dead on the floor. It is thought he was straining on the toilet which caused a tear in an artery.*

There IS an illness called 'Death by Chocolate' but in fact it doesn't kill you – it just makes you sick. It can kill a dog, though, if the dog eats too much. A smaller amount can make it pant and poo – which YOU will have to clean up. It is safest not to give a dog any chocolate.

# NAME THAT TOILET: LOO

Loo is the polite British word for toilet. The word 'loo' goes back to the Middle Ages. The world had forgotten the Roman idea of sewers. They used pots to collect the waste and emptied them into a hole in the ground ... or piled up the waste on the town 'dung heap'.

But you might have used a toilet pot upstairs in a bedroom. Then it was easier to just open a window and empty it into the street. The rain would wash it away. You did NOT want to empty it on someone walking down the street because they'd be upset and may smash your toilet pot over your head.

# MIDDLE-AGES MUCK

The Middle Ages were very smelly times. Most rubbish ended up in the streets. Butchers would kill an animal, sell the meat, but throw the guts into the street.

London had public toilets built over the River Fleet to the west of the city. The toilets were just seats with a hole. They were built on a bridge, so the waste fell into the Fleet.

One writer said…

**Each toilet seat is filled with a buttock. Boatmen sailing underneath had to take care not to be soiled.**

And it wasn't only the boatmen who faced the problem of being hit by poo and pee falling from the sky. Many private toilets needed laws to control them. In 1321 London's council took Thomas Wytte and William Hockele to court. Wytte and Hockele closed off Ebbgate lane and built toilets into the walls of a row of houses.

These toilets stuck out from the walls of the houses so that human filth would fall on to the heads of the passers-by.

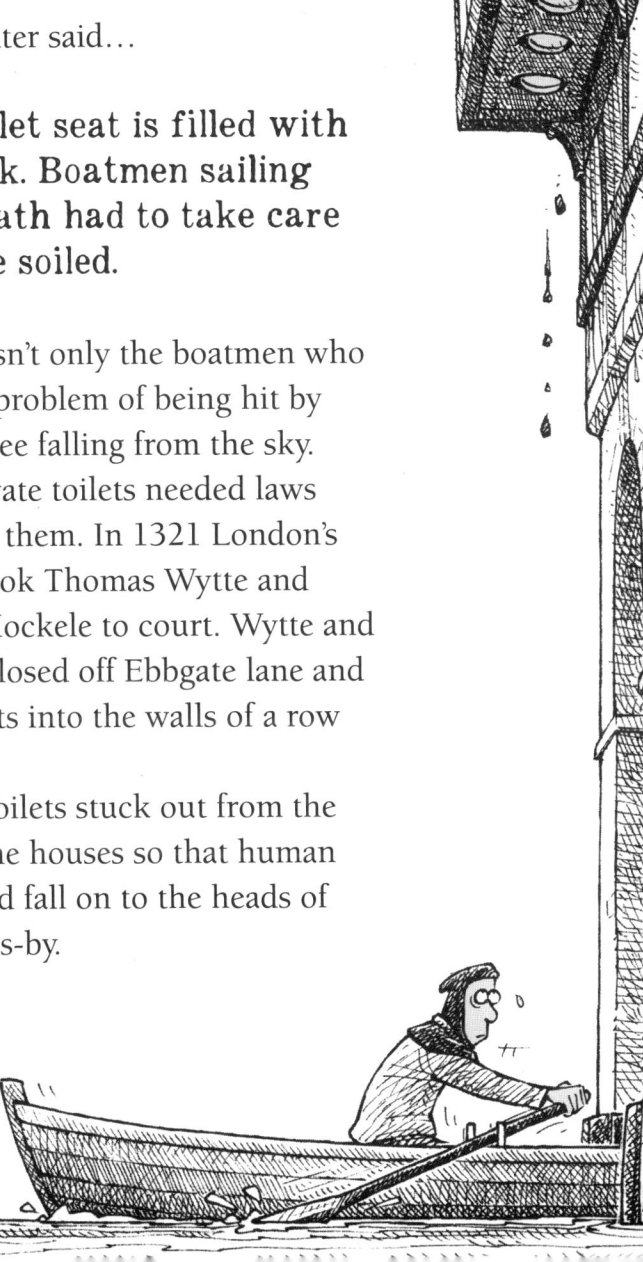

Not everyone bothered with a toilet. They shared a room with animals and behaved like the animals. Even back in 1515 a Dutchman was complaining about the filthy English homes...

> *The floors are commonly of clay, covered with rushes, under which lies an ancient collection of beer, spittle, grease, bones, droppings of animals or men and everything that is nasty.*

Of course, careful housewives collected the family urine because it helped with the laundry. They made their own soap by boiling wood ash with scraps of meat fat. The urine was stored till it was really strong and added to the wash where it bleached material – it made the white cloth whiter.

> **HORRIBLE HISTORIES TIP:**
> If you fancy bleaching your hair then go to the chemist for the bleach. It will cost a bit more than old urine but at least you won't smell like a broken toilet.

In the Middle Ages, most people in Europe did not have indoor toilets. Instead, they used chamber pots or went to the toilet outside. There were no proper sewers to wash away the waste and that led to the spread of diseases, such as dysentery, or cholera in later years.

# DID YOU KNOW...?

Cholera is a little germ that attacks your guts. You get it by drinking water that has other people's poo in it. Or maybe by eating food washed in the dirty water. After a week you let out lots of watery poo. Then you begin to throw up. You turn a blue-grey colour, then die.

A doctor will cure you nowadays. But there was no cure in horrible history.

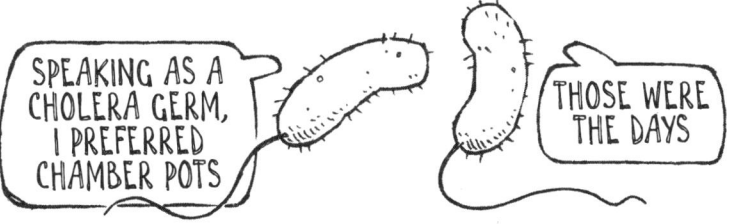

# KILLER TOILETS 3

A man fell in the Tewkesbury toilet trench on a Saturday. He refused to let anybody help him because Saturday was his holy day.

But the Lord of Tewkesbury Manor in 1260 was cruel Richard de Clare. De Clare said:

The man was left to drown in poo.

## TOILET TALES

Once upon a time (the story says), there was a poor and starving boy called

Dick Whittington. He had a cat that made him rich…

The tale is often told as a pantomime. Poor Dick came back to London, married his master's daughter, Alice Fitzwarren, and made his fortune as a trader in silks, velvets and furs. He was made Lord Mayor of London four times.

The Horrible Histories truth is that Dick Whittington (1354–1423) was a real person. He wasn't a poor boy from the country. He was the son of a Member of Parliament. But he DID marry Alice Fitzwarren. She died before him, and he had no one to leave his money to. So, he wanted it used to care for the poor.

He hated London's terrible toilets. He left money to have a new public toilet built with 128 seats. It was called 'Whittington's Longhouse' in the district of Vintry. It was flushed clean by the River Thames at high tide.

London people were better off. But some other creatures were not.

Twice a year (late July and December), the king or queen of Britain gives four dead deer to the Lord Mayor of London. Why? Mayor Whittington loaned money to King Henry V to fight in France (the Hundred Years' War). Henry V won a great victory at the battle of Agincourt. The deer were the King's thank you to (his dear friend) Dick. And the tradition has carried on every year since.

# KILLER TOILETS 4

People would pee in the streets. When it rained the pee was washed away. The trouble was peeing into the street could be deadly ... when you did it from ten metres above the street. A woman lost her husband John Toly that way in 1325. If she had reported it in her diary it may have looked like this...

---

13 January 1325

Dear diary,

It is so cold. No one wants to go to the toilet pit outside in this weather. But my husband John was desperate for a pee. (He had been drinking too many pots of ale in the tavern.) He had staggered home, taken off his clothes and crawled into bed next to me with freezing feet.

'I need a pee,' he said, around midnight. He climbed out of bed and stumbled around but couldn't find the chamber pot. He wasn't going to go into the ice-cold back yard, so he threw open the window and had a pee straight into the street. The trouble is he was still drunk. He swayed forward and fell headfirst on to the cobbles below.

I called the doctor (which cost me a lot of money) but by cock-crow John was dead. I'll have to arrange a funeral. (More money.)

I shall probably die of cold myself. I was frozen in my bed. My miserable, stupid, drunken husband didn't close the window behind him. I hope other women don't have husbands who widdle out of their window.

# GOING, GOING, GONG

In the Middle Ages most people called poo 'gong'. They said they were 'going' (to the toilet). And the word 'going' became 'gong'.

Gong was spread on the fields and the smell could be carried on the breeze into village homes.

# KILLER TOILETS

Some houses had deep toilet pits – or cesspits – under their toilet seat that held lots of waste. In the end they filled up with poo and pee. Then they called in the 'gong farmer' – a workman with a shovel and bucket to empty your pit.

Often gong farmers would work as a team of four.

The gong farmers would sometimes use little children with buckets to squeeze into the narrow cesspits.

The gong farmer would carry your gong on carts to spread over fields. It had to be carried as far away from homes as possible and that was all extra work for the gong farmers.

It could be a dangerous job, as well as a sticky one. In 1326, a gong farmer named Richard the Raker fell into a cesspit. The ceiling above it had rotted and he fell through and drowned.

A gong farmer called John in Preston had emptied hundreds of cartloads of gong during his career. He went home and called into his toilet before he went to bed. His toilet seat was rotten, he fell through and drowned in his own cesspit.

Would YOU like to be a gong farmer? They were only allowed to work at night. Not many people wanted to do it, so the ones who did were well paid. For every ton of gong that they moved they were paid two shillings (10 pence). A gong farmer could make more money in one day than most workers made in one week.

The gong farmers could also find coins or valuables that the house-owner had lost in the toilet pit. And it was never lonely, even for a solo gong farmer.

The trouble was these workers didn't have many friends in their towns and villages. And they were not allowed to work during the day – only from 9 at night to 5 in the morning, so local people would not be upset by the stirring up of stinks.

One London gong farmer broke the rules. Instead of carrying the gong away to tip on to farmland, he poured it down a drain into the River Thames. He was caught and dumped in a barrel full of gong, up to his neck, and put on show in Golden Lane for hours.

Today there are many houses (usually in the countryside) that do not have their toilets connected to sewers. They still use cesspits. These days the gong is sucked out of the cesspits into a tank on the back of a lorry.

Gong farmers are out of a job.

# POSH POO PLACES

If you were rich and lived in a castle, then you had special rooms built called 'garderobes'. A hole in the floor let poo fall straight into the moat below.

But horrible smells filled the garderobe. And the lords and ladies said...

Off you'd go to your posh party. Flea-free.

# POTTY NORMANS

William the Conqueror defeated the English at the Battle of Hastings in 1066. When he died he was ruler of England and Normandy. He left Normandy to his eldest son, Robert, and England to the second-eldest, William – who became William II.

When William II later died, his younger brother Henry became Henry I of England. But Robert had always been trouble and his brothers had never liked him. It started with a toilet pot.

William II may have written in his diary…

> *Robert is such a nasty little brother. Henry and I decided to play a harmless little trick on him. We were in the great hall of the castle playing dice with Robert. We grew bored, so we left the gaming table and crept on to the balcony above. Henry*

*and I took it in turns to fill a toilet pot full of pee (and other stinking matter).*

*Robert was still at the gaming table just below us. We emptied the pot over Robert's head. Robert didn't think it was funny.*

*He flew into such a rage, he attacked us. Our father had to come between us. Robert cried like a baby that dad should punish us, but he didn't. Robert went off to wash and he swore he'd get his revenge.*

Robert's revenge was as foul as that toilet pot. He tried to attack his father William the Conqueror's castle at Rouen in Normandy.

He came face to face – or helmet to helmet – with William and knocked him off his horse. Robert raised his sword to kill the knight on the ground, but William cried out to tell Robert that he was his father. Robert spared his life.

The history of the world could have been changed because of a pot of pee.

# KILLER TOILETS 6

The knights of Europe attacked the Holy Land in a series of Crusades. But these were not always great charges of men in armour on horseback. Sometimes they crept up on enemy tents to murder their foes in their sleep.

On 15 April 1291, a group of Templar knights crept into a Turk camp. One knight seemed to forget that tents are held up by ropes. He tripped over a rope and fell headfirst into a ditch that the Turks used as a toilet. He drowned in the sewage.

# THE DARING DITCH ESCAPE

A Welsh lady called Nest married a Norman lord, Gerald. They lived at Cilgerran Castle, but the Welsh adventurer Owain ap Cadwgan (AD 1085–1116) heard of Nest's beauty and went to visit her. He was so in love that he decided to kidnap her. Lady Nest quite liked the idea.

Owain came at night with a small band of his best warriors to take the castle and kill Gerald. They climbed the walls and entered the castle while the guards slept. When they set fire to some buildings inside the castle walls, Gerald woke up.

He panicked. Didn't know what to do. Nest wanted Owain, but felt sorry for her husband. Gerald wanted to fight the attackers, but Nest said,

DON'T GO OUT, MY LOVE. THERE ARE TOO MANY. FOLLOW ME....

And she led him to a little room ... it was the toilet actually.

As you know, toilets in those days were holes in the walls that you sat on, letting everything fall into the ditch outside. Anyway, Nest stuffed her husband down the toilet hole, he fell into the poo below and he escaped.

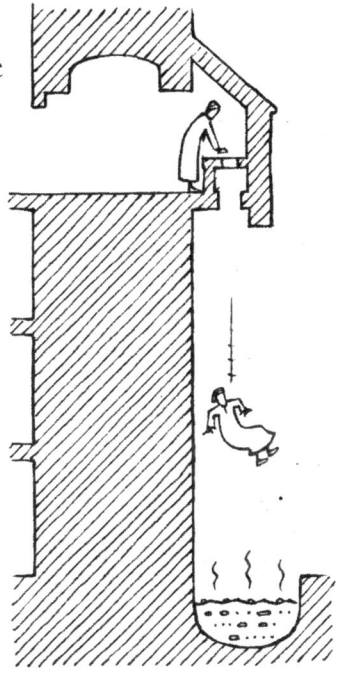

Nest went off with Owain quite happily. The king of England made Owain an outlaw and he had to flee. Eight years later, Owain was murdered.

# SEE THAT PEE

Since ancient times, doctors have treated illness by testing a sick person's pee.

Uroscopy. They would also look at your horoscope and signs in the stars – astrology.

They could then treat chills, fevers, skin and stomach sickness. Doctors were very popular in the Middle Ages.

They would tell you…

If you were sick your doctor would ask you to pee into a clear glass bottle. He would then look at the colour of your urine and compare it to the colours on a uroscopy wheel.

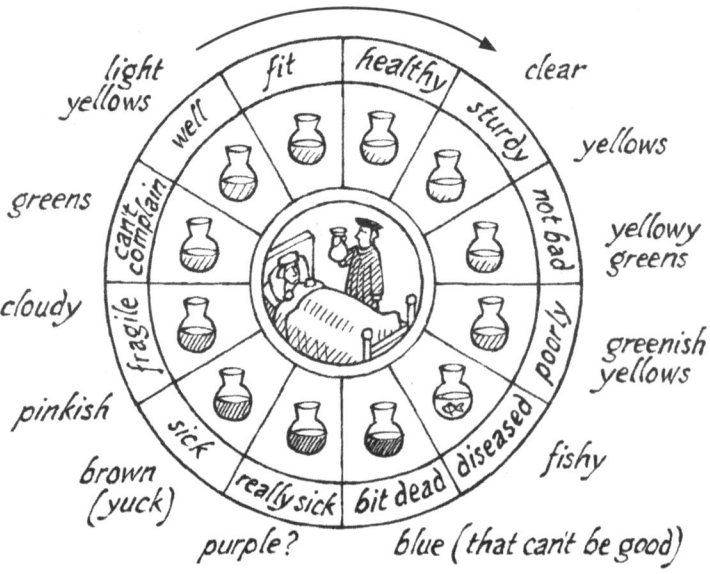

But medieval doctors had a really important test.

And that is what they would do. This went on until around 1800. But even in 1862 Dr William Roberts moaned about the fact that Victorian doctors had given up sniffing urine. He said...

You can learn a lot from sniffing urine. It helps you to know what the disease is and how bad it has become.

Of course, you shouldn't try it because toilet waste can be deadly ... as Queen Victoria may have found out...

# KILLER TOILETS

..................................................................

Queen Victoria married her great love, Prince Albert. They had nine children.

Then Prince Albert died of typhoid fever on December 14 1861 at the age of 42.

BUT there is an old story that the dirty water from Queen Victoria's toilet leaked from a broken pipe into the water that Albert drank. Some history writers say that's what gave him typhoid.

It's a good story, but there is no proof that Queen Vic's poo killed poor Al. It could have been anything he ate or drank that carried the disease.

# KWIK KWIZ

........................................................

Simply answer **true** or **false**.

1 If you live in Scotland and a stranger asks to use your toilet you have to say 'Yes'.

2 The average kitchen chopping board has around 200 times as many toilet-related bacteria on it than a toilet seat.

3 Smartphones have fewer germs than a toilet handle.

4 Air freshener for toilets was invented in 1945 after the Second World War.

5 South Korea has an entire theme park and museum about toilets.

Answers:
1 True. You cannot refuse someone the toilet in Scotland. That's Scottish common law.

2 Horrible but true. Lots of the germs come from raw meat, but that's also one of the reasons you need to wash your hands after using the toilet and before cooking dinner. One person in every five does NOT wash their hands. Grim.

3 False. Smartphones have lots more bacteria than toilet handles. Most desks have 400 times more bacteria than the average toilet seat.

4 False. The first toilet freshener was made from fruit and herbs, a pomegranate stuffed with cloves, and was used well before 1945.

5 True.

# WEE WILL FIGHT TO THE END

There are lots of stories about castles being attacked in the Middle Ages. The defenders on the walls were supposed to pour boiling oil on the heads of the attackers ... but that was unlikely. Oil was far too precious and was saved for cooking.

Water was also valuable if the castle was under siege and the attackers stopped you getting to the nearest stream.

What could the defenders use?

So, even urine was useful in the Middle Ages.

# SOUTH AMERICAN CESSPITS

The Incas in South America were known for some of their unusual customs. One of them was that a boy could call himself a man only after he'd sacrificed a llama.

In 1532 the Spanish Conquistadors arrived and put a stop to those sacrifices. But the soldiers from Europe discovered that the Inca people were superior in another way. They had top-class toilets.

These toilets were pits lined with stone or brick, and they were often linked to drains to carry away the waste.

# TERRIFYING TUDORS

# NAME THAT TOILET:
# JOHN

Some people call the toilet the 'John'. Why? It's an odd story…

The first modern flushing toilet was invented in 1596 by Sir John Harington (1561–1612), one of Queen Elizabeth I's godsons. Elizabeth (1533–1603) banned him from her palace for being rude about a lady-in-waiting. His answer was … a toilet.

If he'd written to Elizabeth, his letter may have looked like this…

21 May 1589

YOUR MOST ILLUSTRIOUS AND
BEAUTIFUL MAJESTY,

It is almost six years now since you banished me from court. I deserved it. The joke I made about Kate Sedley's chest was extremely rude and I quite understand why she was so upset. I also understand why you told me to leave your palace and never return.

But you are my godmother and such a sweet, kindly person, I thought that perhaps you may have forgiven me enough to come and visit me. Let me tell you what I have been doing in the six years that I have been away.

I didn't mean to annoy you. A day without seeing you is like a day without sunshine. I came home to my old family home in Somerset and wept for weeks. Then I decided on my great project. I decided to build a new house, a great house, and a house with an invention so magical that you would have to visit me.

You see, when I built my Kelston Park, I built in a special toilet system. It works with water. The person entering the jakes sits on a comfortable wooden seat. When they have finished, they then pull a lever and water from a tank above the toilet rushes down. The foul-smelling waste is washed away down a drain to a deep pit. The result is the sweetest-smelling house you've ever sniffed.

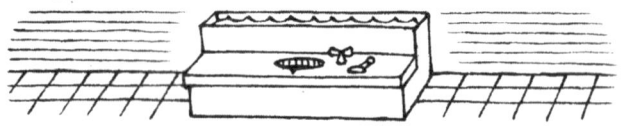

If you will excuse my little joke, I call my invention 'Ajax' after the Greek hero – and because I invented 'a jakes', another term we use for the toilet. Ha. You always did like my jokes, dear Godmother. But please, please come to Kelston Park. Please forgive me and please inspect Ajax.

Your loving godson,
John

Suppose you were Queen Elizabeth. What would you do if you got a letter saying, 'I'm sorry about my rude joke six years ago but, if you forgive me, you could come and see my new toilet'?

What did Elizabeth do?
**a)** Ignore the letter
**b)** Visit John and forgive him
**c)** Have him drowned in his own toilet bowl

**Answer:**
**b)** The Queen was in a good mood. She went across to Kelston Hall in the summer of 1592 and used the Ajax. It is said she loved it. Not only did she forgive her godson, but some stories say she invited him back to London to fit his toilet invention in all of her palaces. Other stories say she refused to use it because it was too noisy.

Elizabeth I liked her 'commode' ... a wooden box with a hole in the top and a potty to catch the waste.

The queen covered her commode in red velvet and lace. Her servants used bunches of herbs and flowers to hide the smell.

Elizabeth was the first monarch in Britain to have a flushing toilet, but it was another 200 years before the idea really caught on and was used in a lot of houses. John Harington made the first. And that is why some people call toilets 'Johns'.

### Can you guess...

Boys at St Paul's School in London in Tudor times had to pee into large tubs. Why?
a) Because it was cleaner
b) Because the school could sell the urine to local leather workers for softening leather
c) Because the toilets in the school were built too high for the infants to use

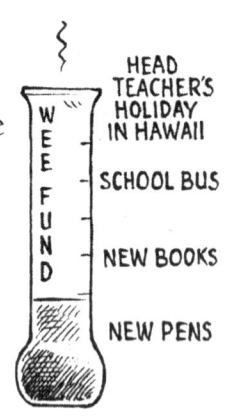

**Answer: b)** The school sold the urine and put the money they made towards the school fund. Your school will have a school fund. Has your Head thought of this as a way of making you a rich school? (Better not suggest it to your headteacher. They may say 'yes'.)

# DID YOU KNOW....?

One gong farmer who emptied Elizabeth I's toilets wasn't paid in cash. He was paid in brandy.

# POOS IN STOOLS

King Henry VIII (Elizabeth I's dad) is famous for eating a lot and getting fat. Put a lot of food in one end and it has to come out at the other end. You need to poo.

Henry's room had a 'stool' – a toilet bowl inside a wooden box, a bit like Elizabeth I's commode. Henry had a servant called the 'Groom of the Stool'. This lucky man had to make sure Henry's potty was always kept fresh and empty.

He also had to help the king to wipe his bottom using a wet cloth. A hundred years before Henry took the throne there was a

rhyme written to tell Grooms of the Stool
what their job involved…

> See that the toilet is fair, sweet and clean,
> See that the stool has a cover so green.
> Make sure the cover lets no board be seen,
> And there's a soft cushion where royal end has been.
> Linen to wipe after moving the bowel,
> Fresh water and basin and carry a towel.

Every king needs a Groom of the Stool. Maybe you would like a job in charge of a monarch's toilet when you leave school?

# GONG ALONG

The Tudor people still needed gong farmers. But some Tudors liked to tip their poo straight from their bedrooms into their cesspits in the ground outside. They had wooden chutes built so the soil would slide down into the cesspit.

Today water parks have slides like that. Maybe Tudor kids enjoyed a cess-slide ride?

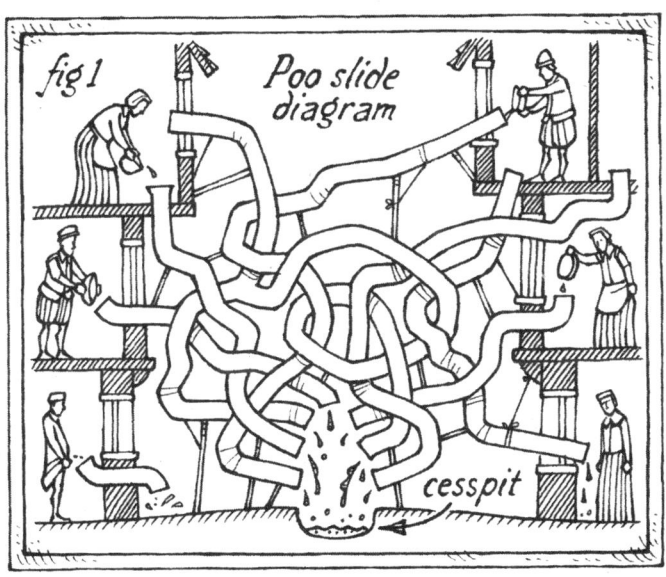

# NAME THAT TOILET: JAKES

Around the time of the Tudors the word for toilet was 'Jakes'. No one is sure why but maybe because the dirtiest sort of person was a peasant … and Jakes was a Tudor word for peasant ('Jacques' was French for peasant). The dirtiest place to go was the toilet.

# THE COOK'S TERRIBLE TALE

A 'laxative' is a herb or a medicine that makes you poo. It is very useful if your bowels are blocked. But you have to be careful not to swallow too much, as the sad tale of the Bishop of Rochester's cook shows…

# THE TUDOR TIMES
*13 Sept 1531*

*CESS MESS?* **WIN A COMMODE** WITH THE TIMES LOO SUDOKU

# COOK COOKED

Richard Roose, the Bishop of Rochester's cook, was executed today in a horrible manner. Readers will remember that Roose was head cook in the Bishop of Rochester's palace. But one day the bishop, John Fisher, annoyed Roose, and the cook decided on a little revenge. He would play a trick on the bishop and his friends when they came to dinner.

Roose found herbs that caused diarrhoea and dropped them into the pot of stew. The bishop and his guests didn't notice anything unusual about the stew … until they went to bed. The herbs began to work on their guts, and they ran to the palace toilets. Bishop John Fisher lived but sadly two of his feeble old guests did not.

Roose was arrested and tortured. He told the truth about the horrible herbs he had used. 'But I only did it for a joke,' he said. The judge did not laugh. He sentenced Roose to hang.

News of the crime reached King Henry VIII and the King was furious. 'Poison? I hate poison. We have to make poisoners too scared to poison anyone. I want Richard Roose to be boiled alive in his own pot.'

The lawyers said that this was not possible. 'The law does not allow us to execute someone by boiling them alive.'

King Henry said, 'Then change the law.'

This was done and today Roose was tied to a rope on a scaffold as crowds gathered to watch. A fire was lit under a cooking pot until the water boiled. Roose was lowered in and out of the water until he died.

It was a very gruesome event, and many people were horrified by what they saw. One witness said that Roose 'roared mighty loud'. He went on to say, 'Many women who were there did feel sick at the sight of what they saw

> and were carried away half dead.'
>
> King Henry is happy that this will be a lesson to anyone who thinks they can get away with poisoning another person.

No one had ever been boiled alive as a punishment before hideous Henry changed the law and Roose is probably the only person ever to have suffered that way.

For five years the punishment for poisoners was to be boiled alive. What a horribly hot happening.

Laxatives can kill. A lesson for us all.

# SHAKESPEARE'S GREAT ESCAPE

In Tudor times, William Shakespeare wrote the most famous plays ever. They were often performed in his theatre, The Globe. That was a wooden building with a thatched roof. Fire was a terrible fear.

People were called to church by bells, while the people of London were called to the theatre by the firing of a cannon.

One day the cloth was blasted out of the cannon and landed on the thatched roof. A fire started and almost everyone got out safely. But one man had his pants set on fire. Beer was poured on him, but one story says some of the men in the audience widdled on the burning trousers. It worked.

# SLIMY STUARTS

# CHEERLESS CHURCHES

In the 1640s the government went to war with the King, Charles I. This was the English Civil War where English families fought other English families and sometimes families fought themselves. That meant lots of gunpowder was needed for muskets and cannon.

One of the main things you needed to make gunpowder was urine – pee.

Urine was collected from places such as public toilets, taverns and stables. It was also collected in churches. How?

a) Instead of collecting money after a service the people would give their pee.

b) The church toilets were joined to gunpowder factories with a pipe.

c) Church services were so long people couldn't hold it in. The women wearing long skirts could discreetly pee on the seats.

**Answer:**
c) Soldiers went around collecting church seats, pee-soaked pews, to make gunpowder.

If you thought collecting urine was bad, some people had to collect sacks full of bird droppings to add to the mix.

The urine was mixed with other stuff like animal poo and straw, and placed in large pits called nitre beds. The urine helped turn the poo and straw into nitrates. The nitrates were then made into crystals called saltpetre.

For hundreds of years gunpowder was made from urine. And in the English Civil War it was made in huge amounts.

It was a horribly dirty job. It's said that hundreds of tonnes of saltpetre were made from urine during the war. That went into over a million barrels of gunpowder.

## ROVING AND RAKING

From the early 1600s the larger towns and cities began to pay 'scavengers' to take away waste and poo from the streets. A lot of this came from cesspits that had overflowed. There were also piles of rubbish and poo known as 'dunghills'. By 1615 the town of Manchester gave work to 19 under-scavengers, or rakers. They had two scavenger bosses.

## PUDDING LANE

In London in Slimy Stuart times the gong on the streets was collected and taken to Dung Wharf on the banks of the River Thames.

It was loaded on to barges and taken to farms down the river. The lane that ran from the city down to the river was full of these great slimy blobs of offal (guts and intestines) they called puddings, mixed with horse dung and human poo. The place was called Pudding Lane.

Pudding Lane became famous. In 1666 a bakery in Pudding Lane caught fire and the fire spread. It became known as the Great Fire of London.

Some history books have said…

But you would NOT want to eat those sort of puddings.

Dung Wharf is gone now. In its place is The Mermaid Theatre. You can go there to see a play and know there is no dung. (And no mermaids either.)

# AWFUL 'OFFICES'

One of the men who saw the Great Fire of London was the writer Samuel Pepys. He didn't call a toilet a toilet. He called it a 'house of office'. He was disgusted by most of London's toilets. When he found a good one he wrote about it in his diary.

> 30 May 1661
>
> I went to my Lord's house, and found my Lord was out. But I went to his house of office. It was in a most beautiful and healthy state. I could not help but notice it.

Other toilets were disgusting and put him in a bad mood. He wrote…

> 20 January 1660
>
> I was on my way downstairs to the house of office, where I saw a scholar ahead of me. I knew he was a very great joker. I could not get past him, so I did give him two or three kicks on the backside and went down.

Pepys could be a bit fussy about clean toilets. His next-door neighbour was not so careful about emptying his cesspit. Pepys wrote…

> 20 October 1660
>
> Going down my cellar to look, I put my foot into a great heap of turds. I find that Mr Turner's house of office is full and overflows into my cellar. This doth trouble me.

A few years after Pepys wrote that, the Great Plague came to London and killed 100,000 people. That made London Council pass new laws to give the people fresh water and better toilets.

The health of the people improved, and the Great Plague did not return. It goes to show that good toilets save lives.

# TOILET HUMOUR

Going to the toilet is not funny. It is important. You should never make jokes about it, but some people do. This is a *Horrible Histories* book and would never make fun of toilets.

Very well. Here are five toilet jokes.

All you have to do is fit the first line to the last line (or 'punchline').

| **FIRST LINE** | | **PUNCHLINE** |
|---|---|---|
| 1 Why did the toilet paper roll down the hill? |  | a) An ig. |
| 2 Why were there balloons in the toilet? |  | b) Dung. |
| 3 What does one toilet say to another? | 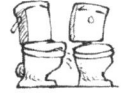 | c) Because there was a birthday potty. |
| 4 What's brown and sounds like a bell? |  | d) To get to the bottom. |
| 5 What do you call an igloo with no toilet? |  | e) You are looking a little flushed. |

Answers: 1d) 2c) 3e) 4b) 5a)

# GORGEOUS GEORGIANS

# YES 'S'

Alexander Cummings (1733–1814) was a Scottish watchmaker who was the first to come up with a new idea for the flush toilet in 1775. John Harington had a toilet that flushed away the waste, but the foul smells just came back up the toilet pipe.

Cummings made a bend in the pipe we call the S-bend trap, which lets the fresh water make a water barrier. Most people call it a 'stink-trap'. It stops sewer gases from rising back into the home.

# NIGHT SOIL GAMES

The Cummings toilets were expensive and in Georgian times not many people could afford them.

Another invention of the Georgian age was steam power. Instead of people sitting in cottages spinning thread and weaving cloth the cloth-making business was taken over by machines – much faster. It changed the land…

🟊 Factories were built around the mighty machines.

🟊 Towns for the workers grew around the factories.

🟊 Those workers needed houses near the factories and the factory-owners built them.

🟊 All those houses had to have toilets, of course. The cheaper the houses and toilets the better.

🟊 One cheap answer was 'terraced' houses – rows of houses joined together.

You'll see these terraced houses were built back-to-back. Why? The answer is toilets.

● Each house had a yard at the back.
● At the bottom of the yard was a box with a hole for a toilet in a outhouse.
● The family used cold ashes from the fire and tipped them into the box to soak up the smells.

But there was a problem...

The back of the toilet box had a door that opened into the back lane.

The night soil men took a horse and cart down the back lanes at night. They opened the toilet-box doors and shovelled the smelly ash on to a cart.

The houses were back-to-back, remember? So, the night soil men could shovel left and right as they drove down the alley and clear TWO streets at once. The night soil carts were emptied over farm fields, just as they had been in the days of the gong farmers in the Middle Ages.

# POO STICKS

If you are a Georgian or Victorian child and you are somehow reading this book (maybe with the help of a time machine), then here is a fun game that you might have played with a friend.

# PUBLIC PIDDLING

There is a record of a man who walked around London with a bucket. If you paid him a farthing (a quarter of a penny), he would wrap his large cloak around you while you piddled. There was no law against it at that time.

He stood at busy street corners or near markets and offered to help people in need. Some people said it was disgusting. A lot of people must have found it useful because he was in business looking after your business for many years.

Public piddling was made a criminal offence in 1986.

# PRIVATE PIDDLING

A Georgian book told readers how to behave politely. It said that when you go out to dinner...

**If you need to go to the toilet then go and return quietly without telling everyone where you're going.**

This was preferred to an earlier dinner habit where pots were kept inside the dining room for anyone who wanted a quick pee. They were hidden behind a screen.

# KILLER TOILETS 8

In Georgian times there were troubles in Ireland because English landowners used the Irish peasants as enslaved people. The Irish rebelled. English landlord Richard Long was caught as he was sitting on the toilet. There was no escape.

Potted on the potty →

There were more troubles in 1916 and the British sent police to keep an eye on the people of Dublin. The police were not popular, and many people of Dublin attacked them. They didn't use guns. They just emptied their toilet pots out of their windows on to police patrols.

Potties on the coppers →

# KILLER TOILETS 9

Sarah Malcolm (1711–33) lived in Dublin. She was desperate for money and knew her neighbour, Widow Duncomb, had a box full of gold.

The old widow shared a house with two maids, old Betty and young Anne. One February morning in 1733 Anne was found with her throat cut from ear to ear. Betty and Widow Duncomb had been strangled. Sarah was blamed.

Her apron was found under her bed, covered with blood. Where did Sarah try to hide her blood-soaked dress? It was found stuffed down the toilet pit.

Forty-five gold coins were found, and they proved she was a thief. Where were the coins found?

a) In her mouth
b) In her hair
c) In her knickers

**Answer:**

**b)** In her hair. Sarah's hair would have been thick and greasy and tied up on her head. She was able to hide the coins along with the head lice. Nice.

# VILE VICTORIANS

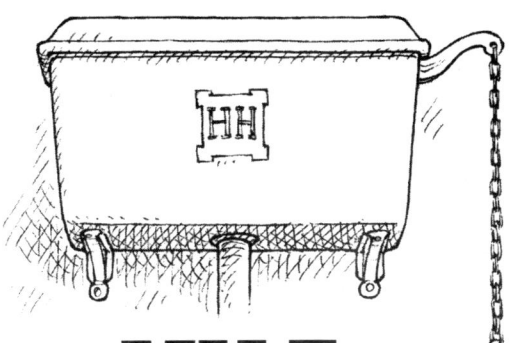

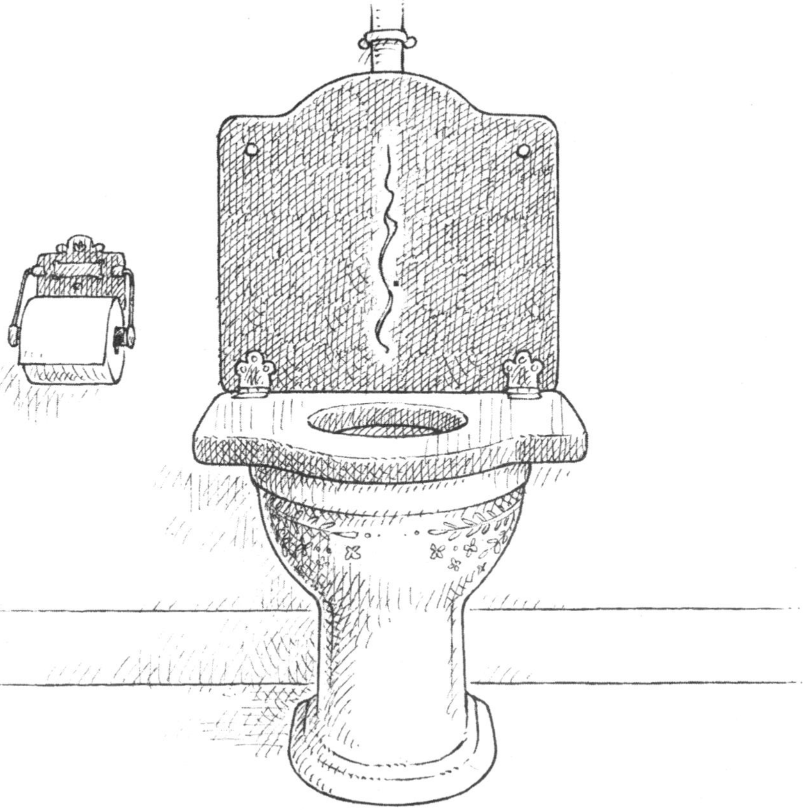

## NAME THAT TOILET:
# CRAPPER

In 1873, Thomas Crapper took Alexander Cummings' flushing toilet idea but made it better. He had a water tank that had a valve – a ball-cock. This gave the water tank just the right amount of water for a flush.

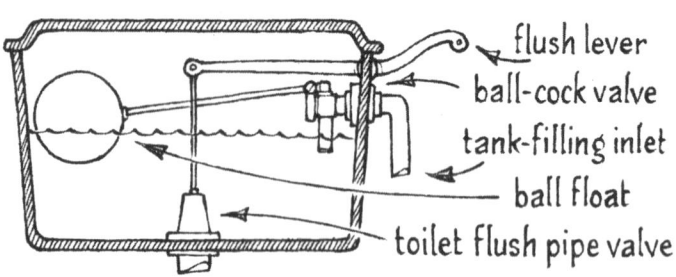

# DID YOU KNOW...?

A toilet flush can throw germs from a toilet up to two metres in the air. Every time a toilet is flushed, germs are lifted into the air and travel around the bathroom. Those germs can land on areas not even close to your toilet, like a toothbrush. The trick to stop this is to put down a toilet lid before flushing ... and then move quickly out of the room.

Queen Elizabeth I had made John Harington's flushing toilet famous. Now Queen Victoria's son, Prince Edward, made Thomas Crapper's toilets a success. He had them put into all of his royal palaces.

Common people (like you and me) started putting Crapper's toilets into their Victorian homes. But in some of the crowded slums around 100 people would share a single toilet. If water was in short supply the toilet would be used many times before it was flushed. Sewage then spilled into the streets and the rivers and found its way back into the drinking water.

Tens of thousands died of dirty water, especially when cholera spread in the 1830s and 1850s.

# VILE VILLAINS

Police had a tough job in Victorian times. They often went to the worst slums to arrest criminals. And criminals could have some very dirty habits. One policeman reported...

> I ENTERED THE HOUSE AND BEGAN TO SEARCH IT. I THOUGHT THE GANG HAD USED THE CUPBOARD AS A HIDING PLACE FOR STOLEN GOODS. I FOUND THE GANG HAD BEEN USING THE CUPBOARD AS A TOILET

# SNOW GOOD

The first big British attack of cholera came in 1831–2 and brought terror to the city of London. People simply fled into the countryside if they could afford to. The poor just stayed and died.

Thomas Hawkins (1810–89) wrote in 1834…

> The first of January 1832 is sadly important as the day in which one of the morning papers wrote 'The Scourge' is present in Southwark; who will ever forget the panic that followed; London was almost deserted in 24 hours. Six hundred cases were counted along the south bank of the Thames – in those crowded lanes where so many Irish people herd, bottled up like a leper hospital.

The clues are there: crowded slums and toilets flowing into drinking water, so the drinking water was brown. That was the breeding ground for the disease. But in those late Georgian days no one made the link between cholera and toilets.

A few people DID notice that the night soil men, who emptied the toilet waste, seemed to live long and healthy lives. We know that's because their bodies grew used to toilet waste. One of the people to see the link between bad toilets and disease was Dr John Snow.

By 1854 Queen Victoria was on the throne and cholera returned. Dr Snow set out to show that cholera was usually carried in the water supply.

Then he made a great discovery…

John Snow had a simple answer.

A report said that bad habits in those mean streets were a gift to the disease. Henry Mayhew wrote that report and called it 'A Visit to the Cholera District of Bermondsey'.

'As we gazed in horror we saw a little child lower a tin can with a rope to fill a large bucket that stood beside her. The family put the mucky liquid to stand. After a day or two the filth and disease has sunk to the bottom, and they skim the water from the top. In this wretched place we were taken to a house where a baby lay dead of the cholera. We asked if they really did drink the water. The answer was, 'They had to drink from the ditch, unless they could beg for a pailful or steal a pailful of water.'

Fifty-four people from London's slums wrote to *The Times* newspaper in 1849 about their terrible toilets – or 'privies' as they called them. Cholera must have affected their spelling too.

They wrote...

> Sir,
> We live in muck and filth. We ain't got no privez, no dustbins, no water splies and no drain or suer in the whole place. If the colera comes Lord help us.

# KILLER TOILETS

# DID YOU KNOW...?

When water from the 1928 flood filled the Tower of London moat, that moat had been empty since 1845. Over the next 80 years the moat had been filled with Tower toilet waste. The flood water turned all that the poo and pee into a filthy soup. Disease killed some of the soldiers and put 80 more in hospital.

# NAME THAT TOILET: DUNNY

The Georgians had begun to send British prisoners to Australia as a punishment. By Victorian times many Brits had settled in Australia and come up with a lot of their own words. One of their words for a toilet was a 'dunny' ... the word evolved from 'dunnekin' which came from dung and 'ken' (house).

The problem Australians faced on the dunny was the redback spider. These spiders can give a very nasty bite on the butt and make you feel sick and sweaty. Up until 1950 they could kill you. Then doctors came up with an antidote to the venom. You still have to get to a doctor quickly if you are bitten, but nobody dies from the redbacks these days.

# DID YOU KNOW...?

One of the great Victorian poets was Alfred Tennyson. Tennyson amused his friends by sitting down and pretending to be someone on a toilet. True or false?

**Answer:**
True.

# NAME THAT TOILET: HEAD

The old navy sailing ships that carried convicts to Australia had a healthy idea for toilets. These toilets were placed at the 'head' or bow of the ship. The water splashing up from the ocean would clean the area. Head has been used in this way since the early 1700s. So if you said you were 'going to the head' it meant you were going to the toilet.

# THE FIRST AND SECOND WORLD WARS

In 1914 the First World War started and went on for four years. Enemies in France dug trenches so they could shelter from bullets from enemy rifles and machine guns.

Behind the trenches there were big guns firing shells that could drop into trenches on the other side.

The answer was to dig a shelter deep into the ground. These holes were called 'dugouts' and could hold ten soldiers or more. The men could eat and sleep there. But there were rules against having a pee in the trench. So, what could you do? Of course, they couldn't have a toilet in the dugout.

For toilets – or as the soldiers called them, 'latrines' – they would build a small hut over a hole in the ground a few metres behind the trench. Or there would be buckets.

A soldier mustn't upset the sergeant or...

Some soldiers crept out after dark to empty toilet buckets. They lit a cigarette to hide the smell from the buckets. Enemy snipers were just waiting to aim at the glow of a cigarette end.

After a few days in the trenches soldiers would take a break a few miles away from the shooting.

Even sitting in the toilet shed just behind the trenches was dangerous. The enemy knew men used these toilets when they woke up in the morning. They liked to drop a few shells among the toilet huts to catch the soldiers with their pants down.

# GERMAN GERMS

A German writer wrote about how good it was being out of the trenches.

What would you enjoy most? Sleeping? Writing letters to your family? Cleaning your toenails? Not Erich Maria Remarque, the author of the famous book, *All Quiet on the Western Front*. Erich wrote:

> The old soldiers don't use the nasty, indoor, common toilet, where 20 men sit side by side in a line. If it is not raining, they use the separate square wooden boxes with carrying handles on the sides. They pull three into a circle and sit there in the sun all afternoon, reading, smoking, talking, playing cards.
>
>

Germans tried hard to keep their trenches as clean as possible. Dirty toilets could give you a disease called dysentery.

That meant…

- pain in the guts
- painful pooing
- bloody poo
- sickness
- fever

# TERRIBLE TOILET TALE 1…

Army boots had to be tough to keep out the mud and water and march dozens of miles. The trouble was the leather was so hard it gave men blisters. Old soldiers knew the answer…

You probably won't want to try this with your new school shoes. But, if you do, remember to empty them before you put them on.

# DID YOU KNOW...?

A soldier usually makes over a kilo of poo and pee each day. For an army company in the trenches this was a tonne a week.

# TERRIBLE TOILET TALE 2...

In the Battles in Flanders in 1917 many troops didn't have proper trenches, just shell holes. They put up a few sandbags to keep out enemy bullets. There were no toilet huts. One British officer moaned...

> *If you wanted to do your daily job of urinating and the rest, there was an empty bully-beef tin, and you had to do that in front of all your men, and then chuck the contents (but not the bully-beef tin) out over the back.*

He forgot to say the REALLY important thing. Find out which way the wind was blowing first.

# NAME THAT TOILET: NETTY

In the north-east of England the poorest houses had holes in the ground for toilets. The name the people gave to these 'earth closets' was 'netty'. This might be from the Italian word 'gabinetti' meaning 'cabinets', a word also used for toilets.

# WOMEN'S WAR WOES

Britain created its first women police officers during the First World War. One of their duties was to stop women workers taking explosives out of the factories, and to stop them taking cigarettes or matches into the factories. Police officer Greta East kept a diary of her life on duty at a South Wales munitions factory. One of her diary pages described the underground toilets they had to use...

> *There are no drains because the ground is below sea level. The result is the toilets are a horrible and smelly swamp. There were no lights in the lavatories and those same lavatories are often full of rats and very dirty. The girls are afraid to go in.*

With no lights, how did you find the toilet paper? Or how did you avoid reaching out for toilet paper and picking up a rat by mistake? Yeuch.

# TOILET PAPER

A woman was sent to spy on Germany in the Second World War. The Germans caught and examined her. They were sure they had found a secret message printed on her bottom.

The woman was 72 years old and was known as 'Madame'. She went to the toilet on a hot train trip to Paris. The toilet was disgusting so she spread newspaper on the seat. The print from the paper stuck to her bum.

German spy-catchers were checking everyone ... and everywhere. They were sure they had caught a spy when they saw the print. They let her go when they worked out what had happened.

# NAME THAT TOILET: TOILET

Using the word 'toilet' itself is quite new. It comes from the French word 'toile', which means 'cloth'. This is because the word 'toilet' was used to describe a cloth that was used to cover the body while you were dressing or bathing. The word came to be used for the room – the room-where-you-cover-yourself-with-a-cloth. In time it came to mean the toilet itself.

# NAME THAT TOILET: JERRY

Before people had indoor toilets they had large pots. These pots were originally known as Jeroboams – and the name became shortened to Jerry. During the First World War (1914–18), the British soldiers looked at the helmets of the German soldiers and thought they looked like Jerry pots. They called the Germans 'Jerries'.

# NAME THAT TOILET: THUNDERBOX

A thunderbox is an old-fashioned word for an outdoor toilet. It was usually a small wooden shed with a seat over a box on the ground. And the sound created inside the shed would echo around the box like thunder.

# TERRIBLE TOILET TALES

A report from 2011 said that around 100 people in the world die from toilet accidents each year. The most common toilet killers are falls, drownings and being electrocuted.

Toilet accidents are more common than you may think. Around 40,000 people get hurt in toilet-seat-related accidents every year in America.

✺ Most toilet deaths happen from falling off the toilet or young children drowning.

✺ Adults suffer bruised bums and tail bones, as well as dislocated hips from unexpectedly sitting on the toilet-bowl rim because the seat is up or loose.

✺ Another danger is being pinched by splits in plastic seats or by splinters from wooden seats. Sometimes the whole toilet collapses under the weight of the user.

✺ Older high-tank cast-iron water-holders were above the head. They have been known to come away from the wall when the chain is pulled to flush.

✺ There are injuries to people who stand on toilets to reach a height, then slip and fall.

✺ There are cases of people slipping on a wet bathroom floor or stepping out of a bath and smacking their head against the toilet.

Other injuries have been caused by animals.

In Thailand a man was using a toilet hole in the ground. He didn't notice a python was having a nap in the hole. The python was not happy. It rose from its comfy bed and bit the man on the behind. The good news is the man lived. Even better news ... so did the python.

There are stories of rats climbing up from sewers to pop up their heads over the toilet bowl. Experts say this is probably not true. If you find a rat in your toilet it would have dived in from above for a drink or a swim.

# EXPLODING TOILETS

In 2012 many American and Canadian toilets had high 'power-assist' to help the toilets flush. But sometimes the high-pressure bit was so high-pressure that the toilet exploded and injured people.

The Victorians had a fear of exploding toilets, although this hardly ever happened. The worriers said…

IF YOU PUT FLAMMABLE LIQUID DOWN THE TOILET AND SET IT ALIGHT, YOU COULD HAVE A FIRE!

# HISTORIC HORRORS

History says quite a few well-known people died on the toilet ... but those stories may not be true:

* Duke Jing of Jin in China (581 BC). He had a nightmare after his personal fortune-teller said he would die soon, and he did. He fell into a full toilet pit and drowned.

*THERE'S A LOT OF DROWNING IN POO IN THIS BOOK*

* In AD 217 the Roman Emperor Caracalla killed his brother then went on to murder 12,000 of his brother's supporters. He was not popular. Caracalla was on a journey with his bodyguards when he said he wanted to stop to pee into a ditch. The guards all turned their backs – very polite. But one guard, Julius Martialis, took the chance to assassinate the emperor mid-pee.

🟥 In AD 336 there was a priest called Arius who founded the Arian Christian heresy. He went to a public toilet because he had a gut problem. But his gut exploded and probably made a right mess on the toilet floor. Someone with a good mop would have had to clean it up.

🟥 In 818, Al-Fadl ibn Sahl, a vizier (high official in Muslim countries) was found dead in his toilet in a palace in the country we now call Iran. He may have been poisoned or strangled. His death may have been planned by his servants or his brother.

🟥 Pope Leo IX (died 1054), who may have been poisoned. He tried to change the Catholic church and made enemies. But the stories of him dying on the toilet – or being poisoned – may not be true.

> POISONED OR ON THE TOILET OR POISONED ON THE TOILET, OR EVEN POISONED BY A POISONOUS TOILET, I DEFINITELY DIED

🟥 Godfrey the Hunchback was Duke of Lower Lorraine (where Belgium and the

Netherlands is today). He was murdered in 1076 when he went to stay in the Dutch city of Vlaardingen. His assassin made sure which of the toilets, built into the walls, belonged to the duke's sleeping room. The killer lurked underneath. When the duke's bottom appeared, the murderer struck up with a spear. It took the duke several days to die.

🏵 Empress Matilda of England (died 1167) may have been poisoned by her husband and possibly died on the toilet (but that story was told long after her death and probably isn't true).

🏵 The Erfurt latrine disaster of 1184 caused the death of at least 60 people, most of them nobles. They went to a great meeting in the Petersberg Citadel, Germany. There were a lot of large men in attendance, and the floor above the toilet pit was very weak. The floor cracked and the lords fell into the poo where they drowned.

✹ In 1892 a man known as J.W. the 'Balloon Man' was famous for his huge stomach caused by constipation. He went to the toilet and was found dead in there. His guts are now on display at the Mütter Museum in Philadelphia.

✹ In 1945, the German submarine U-1206 crept around the Atlantic, sinking enemy ships. It was near Scotland when a toilet fault let seawater flood into the hull. It reached the sub's batteries and that made chlorine gas. The poison gas would kill the crew, so they surfaced for fresh air. A British aircraft spotted them so they climbed into life rafts and rowed away before they were bombed. Some people blamed the captain, Karl-Adolf Schlitt.

🟣 Air Canada Flight 797 was destroyed in 1983, with 23 people dying in the crash. A fire started at the rear of the plane near the toilet.

🟣 Michael Anderson Godwin was a murderer. The court in South Carolina was going to send him to be executed by electric chair. The judge changed that to life in prison instead. But, Godwin sat on the metal toilet in his cell while fixing his television. He bit into one of the wires, and the electric shock killed him.

Of course, none of these stories are as much fun as the toilet deaths in fiction. In the 1993 movie *Jurassic Park* Donald Gennaro is eaten by a Tyrannosaurus rex while sitting on the toilet.

# TOILET ROLLS

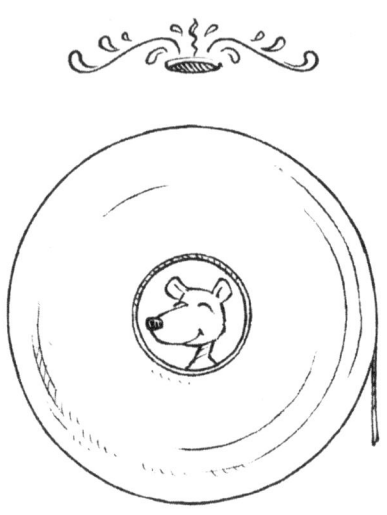

The Romans had sewers and now every town has them. They keep the streets clean. But how do humans keep themselves clean?

In the world three out of every ten people use toilet paper. A lot of people in southern Europe, Africa and Southeast Asia use water instead.

How much do YOU know about cleaning up after using the toilet? Try this quick quiz.

# WIPING WONDERS

1 What was the horrible problem with toilet paper in the 1930s?
a) It was too soft so your fingers went through it.
b) It was too hard so you scratched yourself.
c) The paper had wooden splinters in it ... ouch.

2 A Stone Age body was found in ice. What was the man carrying in his bag to use as toilet paper?
a) Toilet paper
b) Moss
c) A rat

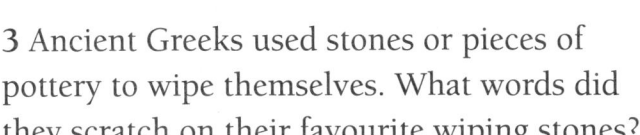

3 Ancient Greeks used stones or pieces of pottery to wipe themselves. What words did they scratch on their favourite wiping stones?
a) Their name so nobody could pinch the stone.
b) A prayer, 'Bless this mess'.
c) The name of an enemy.

4 Where in history was toilet paper first used?
a) China
b) Australia
c) Mumbai

5 Early settlers in America used a common food to wipe themselves. What?
a) Corn on the cob (using just the cob after the corn had been eaten).
b) Peas still in their shells (NO. Not pees).
c) Yorkshire puddings (while they were still warm and soft).

6 In Europe today who uses the most sheets of toilet roll?
a) Donkeys
b) Men
c) Women

**7** Vikings sailed the world in their longboats. What part of the ship did they use to wipe?
a) Oars
b) Sail-cloth
c) Anchor rope

**8** How many people in the world still poo in the open air?
a) A thousand
b) A million
c) A billion

**9** Americans now use enough toilet paper each year to stretch how far?
a) All around Earth.
b) To the Moon and back.
c) To the Sun and back.

**10** How much of your life will you spend on the toilet?
a) Three years
b) Three months
c) Three weeks

**Answers:**

1c) The paper was made from wood that was pulped. But the makers didn't do a very good job and left splinters in some of their toilet rolls. A 1935 'Northern Tissue' advert said...

---

**BE KIND TO YOUR BEHIND**

Northern Tissue toilet paper has NO splinters.

Squat then blot your bot
without a spiky spot

---

2b) Early humans used stones to wipe themselves. The used stones were then thrown into a river. But the ice-man had carried a bag of woven grass and inside was a lump of moss. Warmer and softer than stones.

3c) It's a nice idea. Wiping your bottom on your enemy's name. Sadly, writing your evil teacher's name on a piece of today's toilet paper could smudge.

4a) We don't know exactly when toilet paper was first used. But an Arab explorer went on his travels to China in AD 851. He wrote that the Chinese were using paper instead of water.

5a) Corny but true. The early settlers from Europe also used straw.

6b) Men use an average of 8.1 sheets and women use 6.3 sheets. If you answered a) Donkeys, then you are an ass. The average person uses 85 rolls of toilet paper each year.

7c) Vikings used old or damaged anchor rope as their toilet paper. They also used the shells of shellfish to wipe their bums and so did the fishermen in old Britain.

8c) There are 8 billion people in the world. The World Toilet Organization say one billion people in the world go to the loo outside. So, one person in eight will poo outdoors.

**9c)** Americans use 433 million miles (697 million km) of toilet paper each year, which is enough to stretch from Earth to the Sun and back.

**10a)** Most people visit toilets about 2,500 times a year. That's about seven times a day, or an average of three years on the toilet in a lifetime.

# DID YOU KNOW...?

In the Second World War the British had spies who would be dropped by parachute on to enemy land. These spies took over an airfield at Harrington. Royal Air Force pilots had flown from Harrington and were fond of the airfield. When they were forced to move out they took their revenge: they bombed the spies … with hundreds of toilet rolls.

Ten thousand years ago human waste was not really a problem. There were only about five million humans on Earth and their poos and pees could be buried or thrown in rivers or used to help crops.

Then towns grew bigger. Most were built near a river and the river could carry away the waste. The problem was getting the waste to the river without having to carry it. Messy.

For more than 2,000 years humans have thought that washing their waste away from their homes is a good idea. They invented 'sewers'.

YOU KNOW THE OLD SAYING – 'OUT OF SIGHT, OUT OF NOSTRILS'

# DID YOU KNOW...?

Some of the earliest sewer systems were made around 3000 BC in the ancient cities of Harappa and Mohenjo-daro (that is Pakistan today). The simple sewers were carved in the ground alongside buildings.

The Romans came up with their famous sewers but then the world seemed to forget about them for more than a thousand years.

People in towns and cities used cesspits instead. All the waste from a house (as well as a lot of rubbish) was allowed to fall into the special pit.

The full pits were emptied on to the land or into rivers, but cities grew larger. There was more waste than farmers needed and the rivers couldn't wash it all away.

By the middle of the 1800s there were more than 200,000 cesspits in the city of London and flushing toilets dumped tonnes of waste into the river. The problem became too great. It was known as…

# THE GREAT STINK

July and August 1858 were hot months. There wasn't enough fresh rainwater to wash away the sewage, so it lay on the banks of the River Thames and baked. A newspaper cartoon at the time showed Death rowing up the river. He was taking the lives of the foolish people who hadn't paid to keep the river clean.

People were fainting in the streets from the smell. The writer, Charles Dickens, said…

*The Thames was a deadly sewer in the place of a fine, fresh river.*

One man, Joseph Bazalgette had a plan.

Nothing was done. But in 1858 the stink was so bad the ministers and the lords in the Houses of Parliament were choked by the smell. They soaked the curtains in lime, but it didn't help.

Queen Victoria tried to take a pleasure cruise on the Thames but turned back after a few minutes because the smell was so terrible. Now the men with power and money HAD to do something.

By 1861 the newspapers were saying…

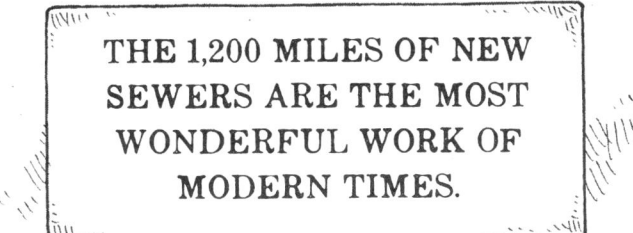

THE 1,200 MILES OF NEW SEWERS ARE THE MOST WONDERFUL WORK OF MODERN TIMES.

In 1866 cholera returned. Another 5,596 people died in the streets from Aldgate to Bow.

A WIN FOR ME

NOT REALLY. THOSE ARE THE PLACES THAT HAVEN'T BEEN CONNECTED TO MY SEWERS. THEY WILL BE

Bazalgette's sewers were a wonder, but with nearly nine million people in London now, they are struggling to keep up with all that human waste.

The Thames became one of the cleanest rivers in the world, but keeping it that way proved hard. Even today heavy rains can send sewage flooding into the river. A storm in 2004 sent raw sewage into the river near Chelsea. More than 10,000 fish died.

# SLOSH AND TOSH

Not everyone thought the filthy banks of the Thames were a bad thing. Some people found the sewer system was a way to earn money. These men, women and children were known as 'mudlarks'.

Some London children made their living by collecting anything valuable that wound up in the Thames. They usually waited for low tide before they waded through the slimiest 'mud' to sort through the treasures dropped in the river. And that mud was full of toilet sewage.

Mudlarks were mostly young boys, although girls and old women and retired men could be seen there too, plodding knee-deep in the

filth. It was tiring work for little reward – a mudlark could hope to find coal, scrap metal, and fire-wood. To find coins or anything valuable was rare.

The two main dangers were:

**1** The '**Toshers**' – the men who hunted in the filth inside the sewer pipes and who weren't gentle in snatching your finds.

**2 Disease** – from any small wound picked up while wading in the poisonous mud. A cut could equal a death sentence.

The water of the Thames gave life to the city folk. But in return they used the river to get rid of their rubbish. They thought it would sail off and sink in the sea, but the heaviest things just sank straight into the mud.

The river became dirtier and poisoned. But in that mud lay treasures. If someone dropped a precious thing down a drain in London then it ended up in the sewers.

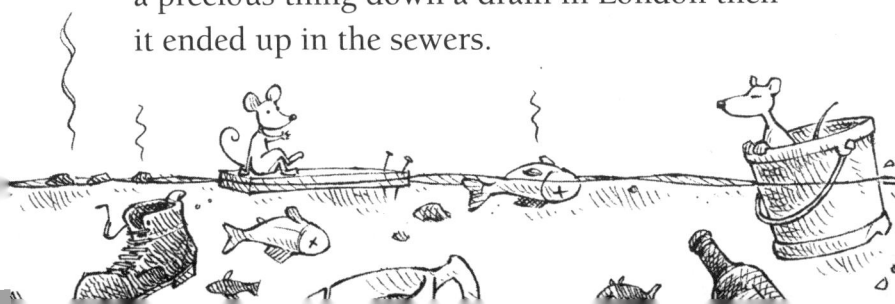

There would be someone there to scavenge for the lost gold and silver. They called their treasures 'tosh' and the seekers were known as 'toshers'. The shores were a foul black porridge.

It was disgusting, working in raw sewage and sometimes finding the corpses of humans, cats and dogs. Broken glass could shred the mudlarks' fingers and let in the poison-water.

One boy told his tale to Henry Mayhew who wrote it in his report 'The London Poor'...

About two years ago I left school and started work as a mudlark on the shore near Millwall. I picked up pieces of coal and iron and copper or wood. I sell the coal and wood to the poor people in the area. Sometimes I make 8 pence a day, sometimes only 2 pence.

Some toshers crept out at low tide to steal the copper that covered the bottom of wooden ships. In 1800 there were more than 10,000 of these river thieves making money from the mud.

Today people still go mudlarking on the Thames to find the remains of history – old pottery and combs, a Roman sandal, a prisoner's ball and chain from the 1600s, and a pot lid from a jar of 'bear grease' ... people believed it was a cure for baldness.

# SAVAGE SEWERS

Toshing was dangerous.

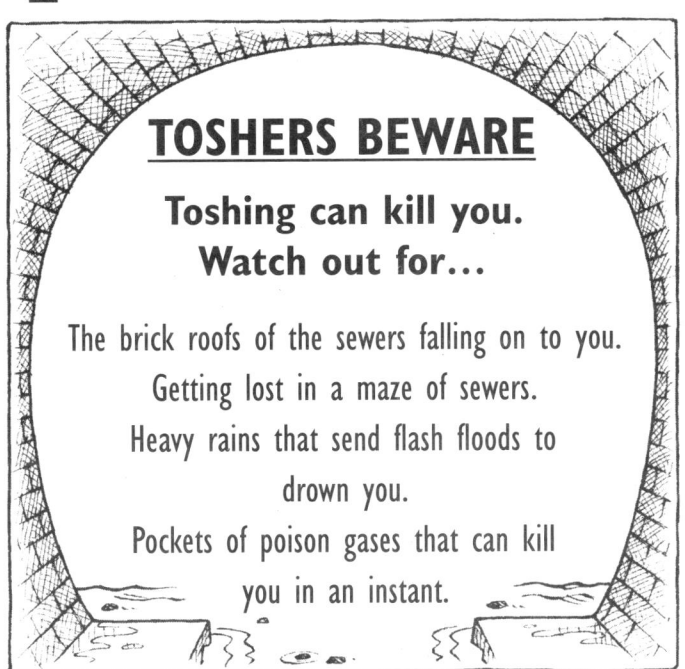

**TOSHERS BEWARE**

**Toshing can kill you.
Watch out for...**

The brick roofs of the sewers falling on to you.
Getting lost in a maze of sewers.
Heavy rains that send flash floods to drown you.
Pockets of poison gases that can kill you in an instant.

# HOME SWEET SEWER HOME

Some creatures have learned that sewers are a good place to live.

# Rats

Sewers make great shelters for rats.

But rats can chew through concrete and wreck good sewers.

# Cockroaches

These insects can live in almost any conditions and would love to greet you if you fancy a trip down a sewer.

# Reptiles

Snakes can slither through the sewage and give you a naughty nip, while frogs also live there.

Sewer-dwelling animals: 1. Jakes snake  2. Bog frog

There are reports of snakes appearing in toilet bowls after swimming through sewers to get there.

# Alligators

Since 1935 there have been many stories, especially in New York, about alligators living in sewers. The *New York Times* had the headline:

---

**ALLIGATOR FOUND IN CITY SEWER**

••••••••••••••••••••••••••••••••••••

Youths Shovelling Snow into a Manhole See the Animal Churning in Icy Water

**HUNTERS SNARE IT AND DRAG IT OUT**

Reptile Slain by Rescuers When It Gets Vicious – Where It Came from is a Mystery

---

That was certainly true. New Yorkers are so proud of this story that 9 February marks the city's annual 'Alligator in the Sewers Day'. But since then, there have been a lot of stories invented about alligators living in sewers. They don't. But there have been reports of alligators found in the sewers in other American cities. They fell in or crept in, but they were not living there.

There are pictures from the TV programme *Good Morning America* that show a true sewer alligator being caught on camera in Florida.

Sewer-dwelling animals
3. Smellygator

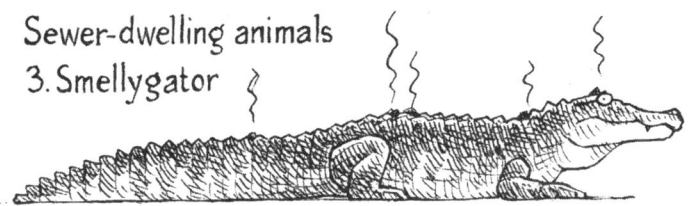

# Fallers

All sorts of animals can end up in a sewer if they fall down a drain. There are reports of foxes, cats and dogs stuck and needing rescue. But the hardest animal to pull from a drain was a cow.

Sewer-dwelling animals
4. Poo cow

# E-PEE-LOG

Toilets are a great invention. They are still evolving: today rich people can buy a toilet seat that can watch users' poop for any signs of illness.

Sadly, not everybody has one. Only around half of the people in the world have a toilet. Some people are just too poor to afford to buy one. They have to manage with the old hole-in-the-ground or a bucket. Toilets that aren't flushed by fresh water are a great hiding place for nasty diseases such as cholera, dysentery and diarrhoea.

AND THE PEOPLE WHO SUFFER THE MOST ARE CHILDREN UNDER THE AGE OF FIVE

Next time YOU use a toilet with flushing water, why not speak to the crapper, khazi, john or dunny and say those kind words...

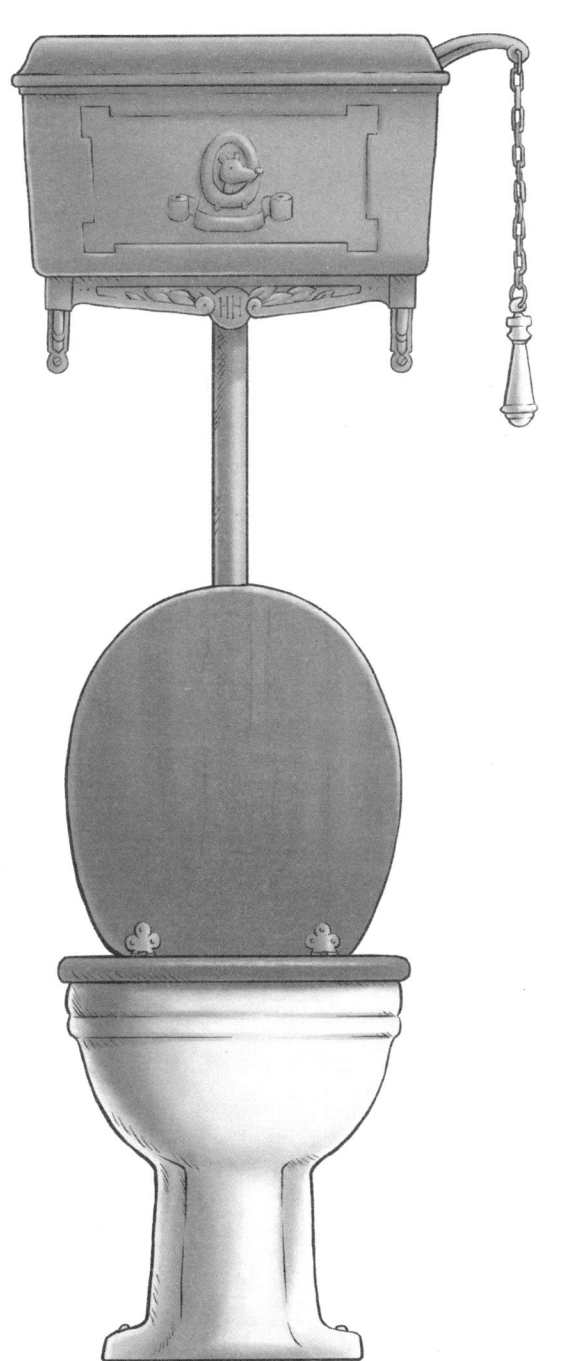

# TERRIBLE TOILET TIMELINE

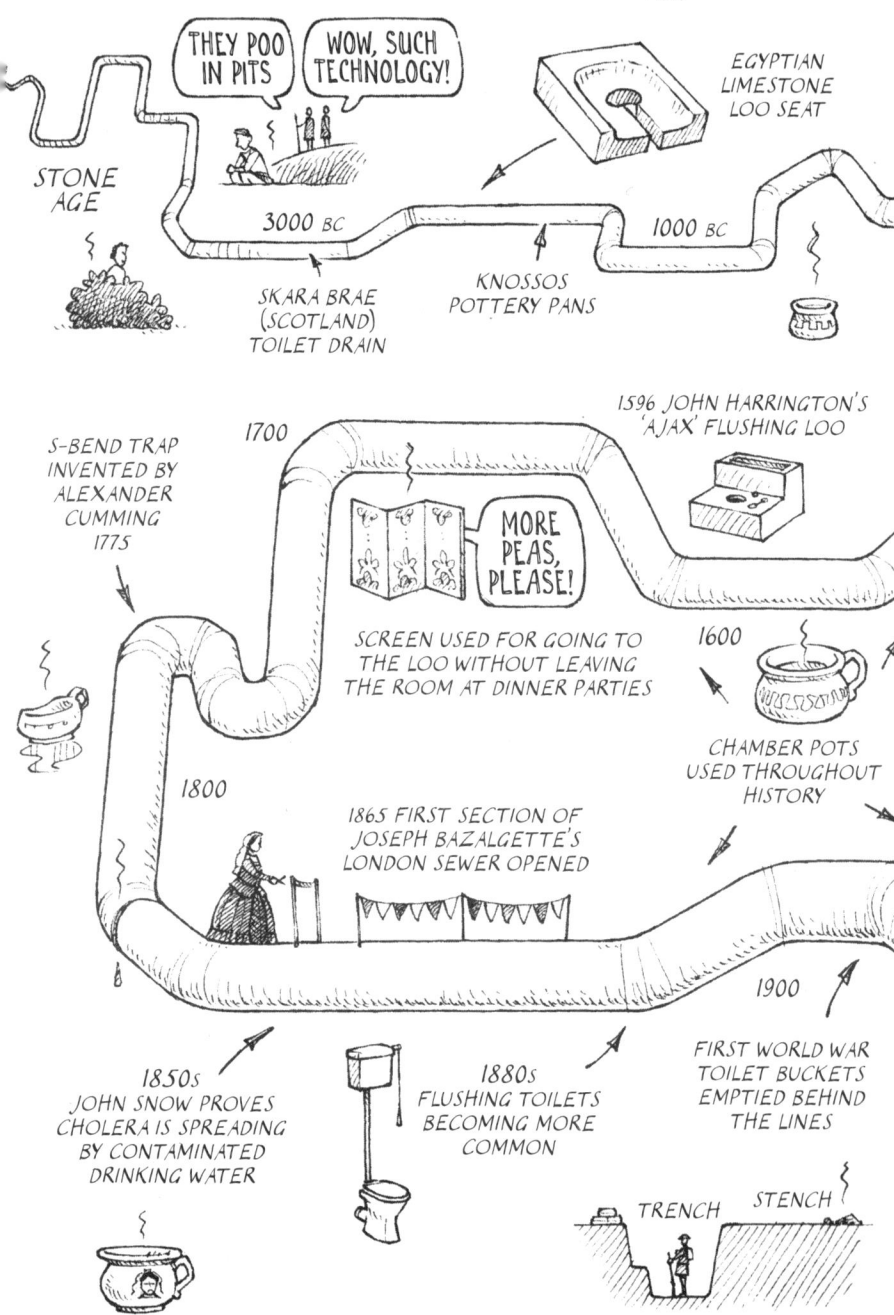

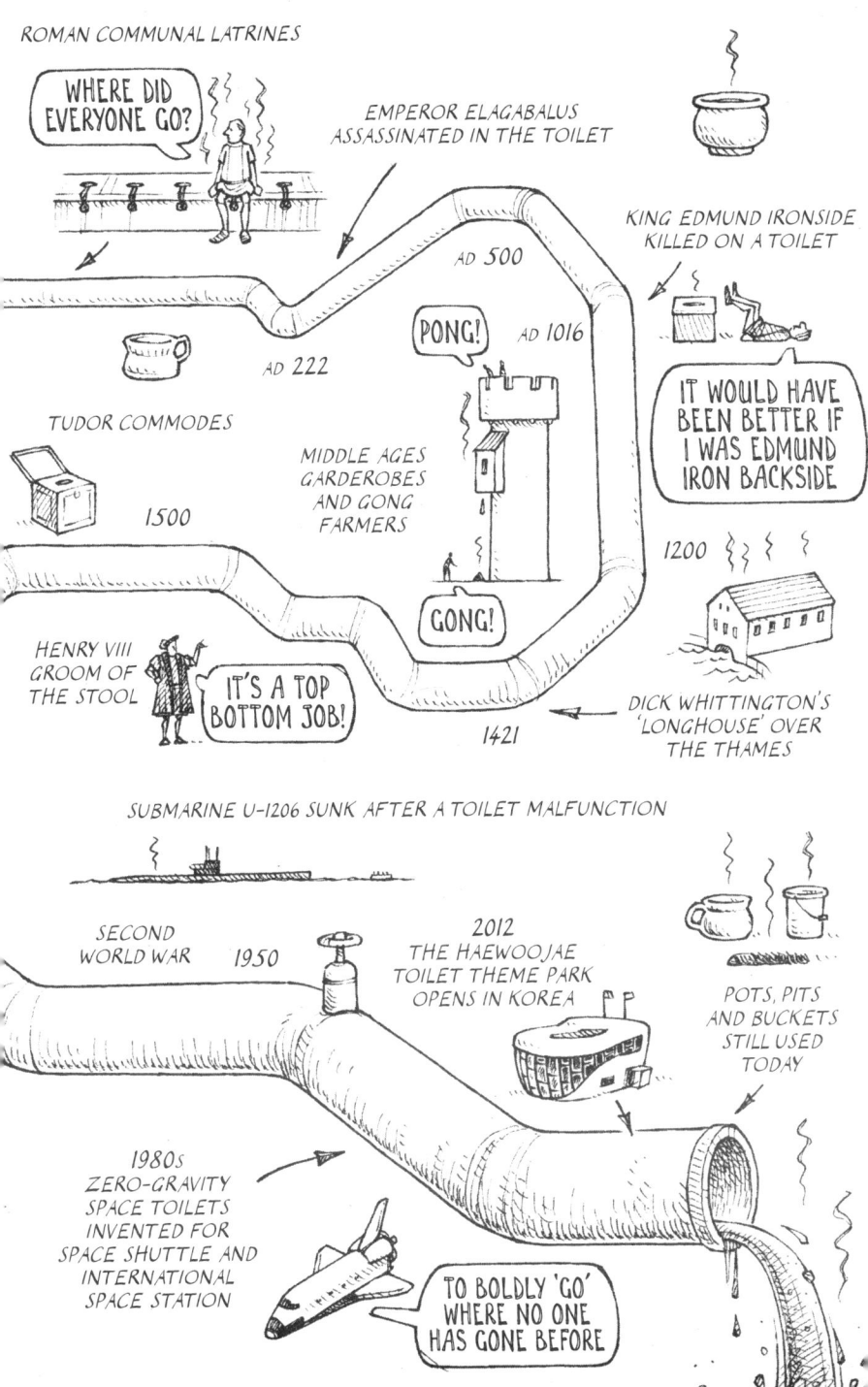

# INTERESTING INDEX

Where will you find cesspits, dung heaps and the Great Stink in an index?
In a Horrible Histories book, of course!

air crash 124
air fresheners 55, 56
Al-Fadl ibn Sahl (Muslim vizier) 121
Albert, Prince (husband of Queen Victoria) 53-4
alligators 146-7
ancient Egyptians 14
ancient Greeks 15, 127
Arius (priest) 121
Australia 101

back-to-back houses 85, 86
Balloon Man 123
Bazalgette, Joseph (civil engineer) 138
bleach 34
boiling alive 70-1
bottom-wiping 16, 17, 65, 66
   toilet paper 125-32

Caracalla (Roman emperor) 120
castle sieges 56-7
cesspits 19, 41-2, 43, 45, 67, 76, 79, 135, 136

Charles I (king of England) 74
chocolate 30, 31
cholera (disease) 35, 96, 97-100, 139, 149
church seats, pee-soaked 75
clothes, cleaning 24-5, 34
Cnut (Viking king) 28, 29
cockroaches 145
coconuts, killer 8-9
commode (toilet) 63-4
coprolites (dried-up poo) 13
cows 147
Crapper, Thomas 94, 95
Crusades (religious wars) 49
Cummings, Alexander (watchmaker) 83

death
  drowning in poo 36, 43, 49, 123
  on the toilet 28-30, 90, 101, 107, 117, 120-4
  see also toilet accidents
Dickens, Charles (writer) 137
diseases 16, 35, 54, 80, 96, 97-100, 101, 108-9, 139, 141, 149
dung heaps and dunghills 31, 76
Dung Wharf, London 76-7
dunny (toilet) 101
dysentery (disease) 35, 108-9, 149

Eadric Streona (English earl) 28, 29
earth closet (toilet) 111
Edmund II (king of England - Edmund Ironside) 27-30
Elagabalus (Roman emperor) 21-2
Elizabeth I (queen of England) 60-4
English Civil War 74, 75
Erfurt latrine disaster 122-3

Etruscan people 18
exploding toilets 119

First and Second World Wars 104-15, 132
fleas 46
flushing toilets 15, 18, 60, 62, 63-4, 83, 94-5, 119
frogs 145
fullers earth (clay) 24

garderobe (toilet) 46
gases 20, 83, 123, 143
George II (king of England) 30-1
Georgians 82-92, 101
germs 16, 35, 55, 95
gladiators 18
The Globe (theatre) 71-2
Godfrey the Hunchback (Duke of Lower Lorraine) 121-2
Godwin, Michael Anderson (murderer) 124
gong (poo) 41
  gong farmers 42-5, 65, 67
Great Fire of London 77, 78
Great Plague 80
Great Stink 137-8
Groom of the Stool 65-6
gunpowder 74-6

hand washing 56
Harappa (Pakistan) 135
Harington, Sir John 60-3, 64, 83
head (toilet) 103
Henry V (king of England) 38-9
Henry VIII (king of England) 65, 70, 71
Herculaneum (ancient Roman town) 14

**holes in the ground** 13, 111, 149
**human sacrifice** 21
**humans, early** 12-13, 15, 127, 130

**Inca toilets** 58
**Ireland** 90-1

**Jakes** (toilet) 68
**Jerry** (toilet) 114-15
**Jing of Jin** (Chinese ruler) 120
**John** (toilet) 60, 64
**jokes** 80-1
**Jurassic Park** (movie) 124

**khazi** (toilet) 25
**knights** 49
**Knossos** (Greek palace) 15

**latrines** (toilets) 16, 18, 106
**laxatives** (drugs) 68-70, 71
**leather, softening** 64, 109
**Leo IX, Pope** 121
**lifetime spent on the toilet** 129, 132
**loo** (toilet) 31, 32

**Malcolm, Sarah** (murderess) 91-2
**Matilda of England, Empress** 122
**Mayhew, Henry** (social researcher) 99, 142
**methane** (gas) 20
**Middle Ages** 26-57
**Mohenjo-daro** (Pakistan) 135
**mudlarks** (scavengers) 140-3

**Nero** (Roman Emperor) 23
**Nest, Lady** (Welsh noblewoman) 50-1

**netty** (toilet) 111
**night soil men** 86, 98

**Owain ap Cadwgan** (Welsh adventurer) 50, 51

**pee**
  gunpowder ingredient 74-5
  peeing out of the window 39-40
  pouring over enemies 57
  putting out a fire with 72
  selling 64
  sniffing 53
  softening leather with 64, 109
  uroscopy (medical examination) 51-3
  washing clothes in 24, 34
**Pepys, Samuel** (writer) 78-9
**police** 90, 96, 111-12
**poo**
  coprolites (dried-up poo) 13
  drowning in 36, 43, 49, 123
  spreading on land 19, 41, 43, 86, 134
**poo sticks** 87
**pots** 19, 24, 31, 35, 89, 90
**public piddling** 88
**public toilets** 16, 32-3, 38
**Pudding Lane, London** 77

**rats** 18-19, 21, 37, 44, 112, 119, 144
**refusing someone the toilet** 54, 55
**Remarque, Erich Maria** (writer) 108
**Robert of Normandy** 47-8
**Romans** 15-25, 135
**Roose, Richard** (cook and poisoner) 69-71

**S-bend trap** ('stink-trap') 83
**saltpetre** (chemical compound) 75, 76
**scavengers** 76, 140-3
**Scotland** 15, 54, 55
**Seneca** (Roman writer) 18
**sewers** 18, 20-1, 22, 23, 45, 83, 135, 139, 141, 143-7
    animals in 144-7
**Shakespeare, William** (playwright) 71
**ships** 103
**slaves** 19, 21
**slums** 96, 97, 100
**snakes** 18, 118-19, 145
**Snow, Dr John** 98-9
**space toilets** 153
**spiders** 101-2
**spies** 113, 132
**sponge-on-a-stick** (for cleaning yourself) 16, 17, 18
**steam power** 84
**Stone Age** 15, 127
**Stuarts** 73-81
**submarine crew** 123
**sulphur** (chemical) 25

**tape worms** 16
**Tennyson, Alfred, Lord** 102
**tersorium** (sponge-on-a-stick) 16, 17, 18
**Thames, River** 137-8, 139-43
**throne** (toilet) 27

**thunderbox** (toilet) 115
**'toilet': origin of the word** 114
**toilet accidents** 117-19
    see also death
**toilet boxes** 85-6
**toilet paper** 125-32
**toshers** (scavengers) 141, 142, 143
**Tower of London moat** 100-1
**trenches, toilets in the** 106-7, 110
**Tudors** 59-72
**typhoid** (disease) 16, 54
**Tyrannosaurus rex** 124

**Vesuvius** (volcano) 14
**Victoria** (queen of England) 53-4, 95, 98, 138
**Victorians** 93-103
**Vikings** 28, 29, 129, 131

**Walpole, Horace** (English writer and politician) 30
**Whittington, Dick** (mayor of London) 36-9
**Whittington's Longhouse** (public toilet) 38
**whoopee cushions** 21
**William the Conqueror** 47, 48
**William I** (king of England) 47-8
**words for toilet** 25, 27, 31, 46, 60, 63, 64, 68, 101, 103, 111, 114-15

# TERRY DEARY

Terry Deary was born at a very early age, so long ago he can't remember. But his mother, who was there at the time, says he was born in Sunderland, north-east England, in 1946 – so it's not true that he writes all *Horrible Histories* from memory. At school he was a horrible child only interested in playing football and giving teachers a hard time. His history lessons were so boring and so badly taught, that he learned to loathe the subject. *Horrible Histories* is his revenge.

# MARTIN BROWN

M artin Brown was born in Melbourne, on the proper side of the world. Ever since he can remember he's been drawing. His dad used to bring back huge sheets of paper from work and Martin would fill them with doodles and little figures. Then, quite suddenly, with food and water, he grew up, moved to the UK and found work doing what he's always wanted to do: drawing doodles and little figures.